Fact Finders®

Amusement Park Science

ENERGY
at the
AMUSEMENT PARK

by Karen Latchana Kenney

CAPSTONE PRESS
a capstone imprint

Fact Finders Books are published by Capstone Press,
1710 Roe Crest Drive, North Mankato, Minnesota 56003
www.capstonepub.com

Library of Congress Cataloging-in-Publication Data
Names: Kenney, Karen Latchana, author.

Title: Energy at the amusement park / by Karen Latchana Kenney.

Description: North Mankato, Minnesota : an imprint of Capstone Press, [2020] | Series: Fact finders. Amusement park science | "Fact Finders are published by Capstone Press." | Audience: Ages 8-11. | Audience: Grades 4 to 6.

Identifiers: LCCN 2018060533| ISBN 9781543572841 (hardcover) | ISBN 9781543575224 (pbk.) | ISBN 9781543572889 (ebook pdf)

Subjects: LCSH: Force and energy—Juvenile literature. | Dynamics—Juvenile literature. | Amusement parks—Juvenile literature. | CYAC: Physics.

Classification: LCC QC73.4 .K388 2020 | DDC 531/.6—dc23

LC record available at https://lccn.loc.gov/2018060533

Editorial Credits
Carrie Braulick Sheely, editor; Tracy McCabe, designer; Eric Gohl, media researcher; Kathy McColley, production specialist

Photo Credits
Alamy: Bill Brooks, 17 (bottom), James Nesterwitz, 11, Serge Bogomyako, 13 (top), 25; iStockphoto: CasarsaGuru, 15, Nikada, back cover (background), 23 (top); Newscom: Image Source/Jon Feingersh Photography Inc., 13 (bottom), Splash News/Duke Energy, 23 (bottom); Shutterstock: Chad Verzosa, 21, Claudio Zaccherini, 9, corbac40, 19 (bottom), KateChris, 20, Krylovochka, cover (bottom), 1 (bottom), Matsuo Sato, 29, Paper Cat, 5, Racheal Grazias, 1 (background), 7, 19 (top), SAHACHATZ, 17 (top), Standret, 27, Titima Ongkantong, 24, Yicai, cover (top)

Design Elements: Shutterstock

TABLE of CONTENTS

CHAPTER 1

ENERGY ALL AROUND!

Put on some comfy shoes and get ready! You're about to enter an amusement park! You'll fly through the air on your favorite rides, scream as loud as you can, and eat some delicious treats. It will be a great day! But have you ever wondered what makes all this fun possible? Energy works behind the scenes all around an amusement park.

Energy is the power to do work. People use energy in different ways. Energy cannot be created or destroyed. But energy can be changed, or transformed.

How is energy at work in an amusement park? Energy can become motion for rides that spin, flip, and dive. Energy can become heat you can feel, light you can see, and sound you can hear.

What are you waiting for? Let's see how energy is involved in all the park's hair-raising thrills!

Energy changes to become motion for rides all over an amusement park.

CHAPTER 2

POTENTIAL AND KINETIC ENERGY

Click, click, click. You're on the biggest, wildest roller coaster at the park. The cars inch up the first hill. It's high—really high! That clicking sound comes from a machine. It pulls the cars up the hill with a cable.

The hill is high for a reason. As the cars climb higher, they gain more potential energy. The cars will use this stored energy to zoom around the track.

As soon as the cars inch over the hill, the potential energy changes to kinetic energy. Gravity pulls the cars down the hill. This force attracts all objects toward Earth's center. *"Aaaahhhh!"* Riders scream and laugh as they free fall. The cars rush up and down the track. They zip around twists and turns. The hills get smaller and smaller. The cars have less and less kinetic energy to move. Soon the ride slows to a stop.

kinetic energy—the energy of a moving object

potential energy—the energy stored within an object, waiting to be released

As soon as a roller coaster goes over the first hill, its energy changes to kinetic energy.

FACT

When you're in free fall, you experience weightlessness. Your stomach feels weird. Scientists think the fast downward rush makes some of your organs move a little. They float up as you fall down.

Pendulum Power

Next up is the pendulum ride, and it's a real rush. The part of the ride you sit in is attached to a long arm. The arm slowly starts swinging from one side to the other. You go higher and higher. Then you loop all the way around before speeding back down.

What's behind this excitement? Pendulum rides build up potential energy as they rise. Then gravity pulls the ride down. Just like on a roller coaster, the potential energy changes to kinetic energy. The ride swings at its axis from side to side. Its energy switches back and forth from potential to kinetic as it rises higher and falls back down. When the ride is at its highest, it has the most potential energy. When it is moving fastest, it has the most kinetic energy. This kinetic energy powers the ride into a full loop.

axis—a real or imaginary line through the center of an object, around which the object turns

pendulum—a weight that hangs from a fixed point and swings back and forth freely using the force of gravity

At its highest points, a pendulum ride has the most potential energy.

FACT

Pendulums often keep time in clocks. Dutch scientist Christiaan Huygens invented the first pendulum clock in 1656.

Slingshot Up!

If you think the pendulum ride didn't get you high enough into the sky, try the slingshot ride! The seats are connected to two cables. The cables go to the top of two tall towers and over **pulleys**. The cables go back down to the ground inside the towers. The other ends of the cables attach to stretchy springs inside a small spring tower near the two taller towers. When the seats are released, you rocket up. You fly past the tops of the towers. You're so high that people below look like ants on the ground!

Hundreds of stretchy springs fling this ride upward. Inside the spring tower, a metal plate is at the top and bottom of the springs. A **hydraulic** system pulls the plates apart. This stretches the springs, giving them potential energy called elastic energy. When the seats are released, the potential energy in the springs becomes kinetic energy. The bottom plate flies up in the spring tower. This pulls on the cables. It makes the seats fly up into the air. The springs and seats bounce up and down. Finally they slow down, and it's time to get off. Whew! You made it!

When potential energy changes to kinetic energy, the slingshot ride's seat launches high into the air.

hydraulic—having to do with a system powered by fluid forced through pipes or chambers

pulley—a grooved wheel turned by a rope, belt, or chain

FACT

Some slingshot rides get the seats more than 350 feet (100 meters) in the air.

CHAPTER 3

THE BUZZ ON ELECTRICITY

Strap yourself in and get ready to drive! Next up are the bumper cars. The cars move in every direction. You stomp on the pedal. *Bump!* You crash into another car. You back up and you're on to the next car. But how do they run?

Bumper car tracks are wired for **electrical energy,** or electricity. Electrical energy comes from **atoms**. Atoms are tiny particles. Everything is made from atoms. Each atom has a positive and negative electric charge. The center is an atom's nucleus. Electrons spin around the nucleus. Usually the electrons stay close to their atoms. But sometimes they move and leave their atoms. When electrons are free to flow from atom to atom, they create electricity.

atom—an element in its smallest form

electrical energy—energy that results from the flow of charged particles, such as electrons, or from a buildup of charged particles on an object

Electricity powers bumper cars as well as many other rides at an amusement park.

AN ELECTRIC DISCOVERY

The ancient Greeks are said to have discovered electricity about 2,500 years ago. But this was a different type of electricity than the one we use today to power machines. The type of electricity the Greeks discovered is called static electricity. It results from a material having too many or too few electrons. An electrical charge builds up on  an object. This is the same type of energy that makes your hair stand up after you rub a balloon against it. The rubbing removes electrons from the balloon and adds them to your hair. The hair's negative charge is attracted to the balloon's positive charge.

Today people make electricity in different ways. One way is at a power plant. The power plant sends electricity through wires to other places, such as amusement parks. Once there, it can be used to power rides, such as the bumper cars.

There are different bumper car systems, but they all use electricity. Some kinds of bumper cars have long metal poles. The poles connect to a grid on the top of the track. Parts under the vehicle connect to the floor. Electricity flows through the grid and the floor. The cars connect to both positive and negative charges through the floor and grid. This completes an electrical circuit. A circuit is a path that electrons can flow through. Electricity flows into the cars and powers their motors. Then a wheel under the car rolls. The electricity is now kinetic energy, and the cars move.

FACT
The first bumper cars in the early 1920s were sometimes called dodgems. They were not made to bump into one another. Instead, drivers tried to avoid crashes.

Bumper cars often have poles attached to them that connect to a ceiling grid.

Electricity Behind the Scenes

Rides get all the attention at an amusement park. Yet they wouldn't work without control systems. Control systems make the rides move and keep them safe. They control which parts of rides get power. Engineers design computers specifically for a park's control systems. Computer programmers make **software** for the systems. These systems all need electricity to run.

software—the programs that tell the hardware of the computer what to do

Because the control systems are so important, a park has generators if the electricity is ever lost from the power plant. A generator is a machine that can create electricity. It uses fuel to move a magnet around a coil of wires. This movement makes a flow of electrons. The generator's electricity can then be used.

A Storm's Rolling In!

Electricity can be in the air at a park too. See that storm cloud rolling in? In the distance, lightning strikes. Did you know that you just saw electricity? In the storm cloud, bits of ice bump into one another as they move around. These collisions build up an electrical charge. The top part of the cloud has a positive charge and the bottom part has a negative charge. When the positive and negative charges become big enough, a giant spark occurs between the two charges in the cloud. We call this big spark lightning. The spark can also occur between a cloud and the ground.

Lightning that reaches the ground is called cloud-to-ground lightning.

POWERING DISNEY WORLD

Disney World is a big theme park in Florida. It covers about 40 square miles (104 square kilometers). That's about the same size as the city of San Francisco! The park uses so much electricity that it has its own power plant. The plant provides some of the park's power through an underground system.

CHAPTER 4

HOT SNACKS, COLD TREATS, AND LOTS OF HEAT

The storm is going to miss us after all. You've ridden on some rides and waited in long lines. Now the sun is high in the sky. Sunlight changes to heat. The air temperatures rise. You're starting to sweat and get a little tired. The fun's not over yet, but you need a break! Time for some snacks and treats. You can see how energy cooks and cools food.

Heat is made from moving atoms. These atoms are in all **matter**. As an object's atoms move faster, its temperature gets hotter. As heat is taken away, the object's atoms move more slowly. Its temperature drops. Heat naturally moves from hotter objects to cooler objects. This heat transfer makes objects change temperature.

matter—anything that has weight and takes up space

On a clear day the sun heats up everything at an amusement park.

STATES OF MATTER

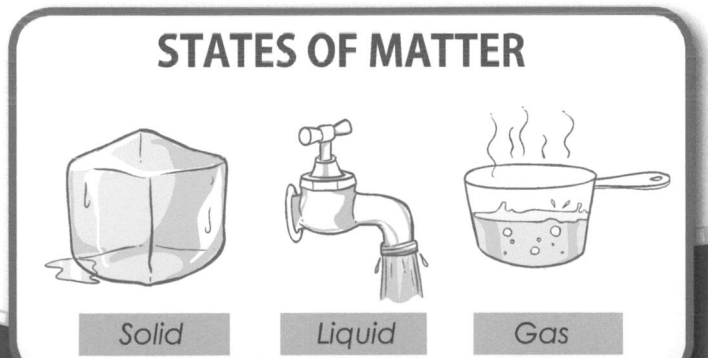

Solid   Liquid   Gas

FACT

The type of matter affects how atoms move. In solids they move slowly. In liquid they move faster. In gases atoms move even faster.

At the park, heat makes the treats you love to eat. Can't wait to bite into that fluffy cotton candy? This super-sweet treat comes from sugar grains. Heat turns the grains into long threads. A cotton candy machine uses electricity to heat up the sugar grains. The sugar's atoms move faster and faster. Soon the sugar turns into liquid. At the same time the machine spins. The liquid sugar shoots out through small holes in the metal container around it. The liquid quickly cools as it shoots out, making tiny threads of sugar. Then the threads are wrapped onto a cone, and it's ready to eat!

Sugar heats up to form cotton candy.

Snow Cone Zone

Maybe you're in the mood for a snow cone. Did you know even cold things have heat? Snow cones are made of shaved ice. This ice was once liquid water. When water goes into a freezer, its temperature drops to below 32 degrees Fahrenheit (0 degrees Celsius).

Heat flows from the water into the air. The water's atoms slow down. They almost stop moving. The water changes from liquid into the solid we know as ice. Shave the ice into a cone and add some fruity syrup. Now you can take a bite!

FACT

Dentist William Morrison and candymaker John C. Wharton created cotton candy in 1897.

Better eat your snow cone fast, though! Before long, your snow cone will melt. Everything's getting hot in the sun, from the sidewalk to the metal bars on rides. Energy from the sun travels through the air as light. We call the sun's energy **solar energy**. When the light hits the planet, it transforms into heat as it hits different materials, such as the ground, air, water, and pavement. It heats up your snow cone too. Atoms move faster inside the ice of your snow cone and it melts. As you devour the rest of your snow cone, your body sweats to help you keep cool. The sweat **evaporates** into the air. It takes some body heat away with it.

---

evaporate—to change from a liquid to a gas
solar energy—energy from the sun

From the pavement to rides, solar energy causes objects at an amusement park to become hotter.

SOLAR-POWERED PARKS

Solar energy can do much more than heat up an amusement park. It can also help power a park. Solar panels gather sunlight and turn it into electricity. The process of using solar panels to make electricity is better for the environment than other ways of producing electricity. Legoland in Florida uses solar energy to power part of its park. In 2018, Disney began building a new 270-acre (109-hectare) solar facility in central Florida. Six Flags Great Adventure in New Jersey also began building a solar facility. When complete, the park will get all its power from the 40-acre (16-hectare) field of solar panels.

Disney's current solar park is in the shape of Mickey Mouse.

CHAPTER 5

BRIGHT LIGHTS AND LOUD SOUNDS

Shouts and laughter roar from the roller coaster. The cars make a loud *whoosh* as they pass by. Lively music cranks out from the carousel. Sounds are everywhere at the park. They travel through the air. Some are loud and some are quiet. Some have a low pitch. Others have a high pitch. What makes these sounds?

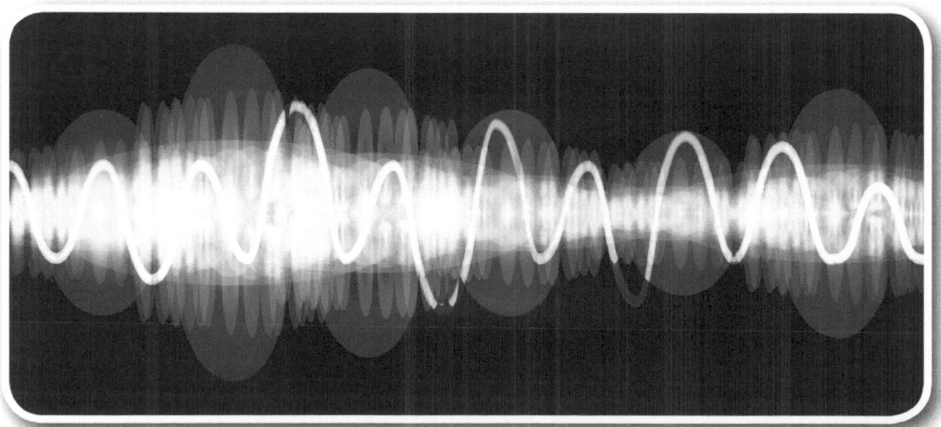

Sound travels through the air in waves.

When an object vibrates, it moves matter. The energy in the vibrating movement transfers into the air. It moves in waves. These **sound waves** move one after the other until they reach your ears. They make your eardrums vibrate. The tiny hairs inside your ears pick up the sounds. They turn them into signals for your brain. That's how you hear all the sounds of the park. The loudness or quietness of a sound depends on the sound wave's strength, or **amplitude**. If the sound waves move slowly, you hear a low-pitched sound. If they are fast, you hear a high-pitched sound.

amplitude—distance from the midpoint of a wave to its crest; a measure of wave strength

sound wave—a wave or vibration that can be heard

As roller coaster riders scream, sound waves travel through the air.

Lighting Up the Night

As nighttime nears, the park lights up. The rides twinkle with bright lights. Colorful lights shine on stages as shows begin. Energy from electricity changes into light we can see.

Light comes from a source, such as a light bulb on a ride or the sun. It's made of tiny parts called photons. This energy moves in waves from its source. It moves in all directions as it spreads out. Light is very bright at its source. It gets dimmer and dimmer the farther it goes.

When light waves reach our eyes, they enter our eye lens. The waves move to the back of our eyes and hit rods and cones. The rods and cones send messages to our brain so that we can see.

Lights from rides shine brightly at night.

FACT

Lasers are a special kind of light. They have waves that line up very closely. This makes the light very bright. The waves create a thin beam of light that travels far without losing much energy.

27

CHAPTER 6

AN EXPLODING END TO THE FUN

Boom! Suddenly lights explode high above you. Red, green, and blue streak across the night sky. A burning smell drifts through the air. It's the end of the night, and this is the fireworks display you've been waiting for all day.

These fireworks are the result of energy stored inside chemicals. Energy is released during a chemical reaction. With fireworks, fire makes that reaction happen. It burns gunpowder. Other chemicals and explosive materials are also inside the fireworks. As they burn, the materials release heat and gas. The heat and gas trigger chemical reactions. The released gas creates a big boom. Mixtures of different metals and salts inside the fireworks determine what color the lights will be as they burn.

Chemical reactions are behind the amazing fireworks displays at amusement parks.

It's been an exciting day at the amusement park. Energy was everywhere. It moved from place to place and changed again and again. From wild rides to tasty treats and loud screams, energy keeps amusement parks filled with thrills.

GLOSSARY

amplitude (AMP-pli-tood)—distance from the midpoint of a wave to its crest; a measure of wave strength

atom (AT-uhm)—an element in its smallest form

axis (AK-siss)—a real or imaginary line through the center of an object, around which the object turns

electrical energy (i-LEK-tri-kuhl EN-ur-jee)—energy that results from the flow of charged particles, such as electrons, or from a buildup of charged particles on an object

evaporate (i-VA-puh-rayt)—to change from a liquid to a gas

hydraulic (hye-DRAW-lik)—having to do with a system powered by fluid forced through pipes or chambers

kinetic energy (ki-NET-ik EN-ur-jee)—the energy of a moving object

matter (MAT-ur)—anything that has weight and takes up space

pendulum (PEN-juh-luhm)—a weight that hangs from a fixed point and swings back and forth freely using the force of gravity

potential energy (puh-TEN-shuhl EN-ur-jee)—the energy stored within an object, waiting to be released

pulley (PUL-ee)—a grooved wheel turned by a rope, belt, or chain

software (SAWFT-wayr)—the programs that tell the hardware of the computer what to do

solar energy (SO-lur EN-ur-jee)—energy from the sun

sound wave (SOUND WAYV)—a vibration that can be heard

To contact Capstone Global Library please
call 800-747-4992, or visit our web site
www.capstonepub.com

Edited by Penny West
Designed by Steve Mead
Original illustrations © Capstone Global Library Ltd 2015
Picture research by Tracy Cummins
Production by Victoria Fitzgerald
Originated by Capstone Global Library Ltd

Library of Congress Cataloging-in-Publication Data
Spilsbury, Louise.
    Pacific Ocean / Louise Spilsbury and Richard Spilsbury.
        pages cm.—(Oceans of the world)
    Includes bibliographical references and index.
    ISBN 978-1-4846-0771-8 (hb)—ISBN 978-1-4846-0777-0 (pb)—ISBN 978-1-4846-0789-3 (ebook) 1. Oceanography—Pacific Ocean—Juvenile literature. 2. Pacific Ocean—Juvenile literature. I. Spilsbury, Richard, 1963- II. Title.

    GC771.S65 2015
    910.9164—dc23   2014010885

This book has been officially leveled by using the F&P Text Level Gradient™ Leveling System

Acknowledgments
We would like to thank the following for permission to reproduce photographs: Getty Images: AFP PHOTO/Robyn Beck, 19, David Wall Photo, 15 Top, Mauricio Handler, 25, Nick Hall, 18, SADATSUGU TOMIZAWA/AFP, 11; Newscom: Jonathan Alcorn/ZUMAPRESS.com, 27 Top; Shutterstock: Anton Balazh, 7, Carolina K. Smith MD, 4, cdrin, 20 Bottom, chungking, 21 Bottom, Dhoxax, 16 Bottom, DmitrySerbin, 14, EpicStockMedia, Cover Top, Fiona Ayerst, 17, Igor Plotnikov, 23, leoks, 12, leonello calvetti, Cover Middle, Naaman Abreu, 22, Tanya Puntti, Cover Bottom, Vlad61, 26 Bottom, Vladislav Gurfinkel, 13, worldswildlifewonders, 24, Zmiter, Design Element.

We would like to thank Michael Bright for his invaluable help in the preparation of this book.

Every effort has been made to contact copyright holders of material reproduced in this book. Any omissions will be rectified in subsequent printings if notice is given to the publisher.

All the Internet addresses (URLs) given in this book were valid at the time of going to press. However, due to the dynamic nature of the Internet, some addresses may have changed, or sites may have changed or ceased to exist since publication. While the author and publisher regret any inconvenience this may cause readers, no responsibility for any such changes can be accepted by either the author or the publisher.

READ MORE

Hawbaker, Emily. *Energy Lab for Kids: 40 Exciting Experiments to Explore, Create, Harness, and Unleash Energy.* Beverly, MA: Quarry, 2017.

O'Donnell, Liam. *The Shocking World of Electricity with Max Axiom Super Scientist: 4D An Augmented Reading Science Experience.* Graphic Science 4D. North Mankato, MN.: Capstone Press, 2019.

Roby, Cynthia. *Discovering STEM at the Amusement Park.* STEM in the Real World. New York: PowerKids Press, 2016.

CRITICAL THINKING QUESTIONS

1. What is the difference between potential and kinetic energy?

2. Read pages 6–9. What type of energy would electricity change to once it powers a motor to make a machine move?

3. Sound moves in waves from a source. Why do you think sounds are quieter the farther you are from their source? Why are they louder when you are closer to the source?

INTERNET SITES

Energy in a Roller-Coaster Ride
https://www.pbslearningmedia.org/resource/hew06.sci.phys.maf.rollercoaster/energy-in-a-roller-coaster-ride/

How Do Roller Coasters Work?
https://wonderopolis.org/wonder/how-do-roller-coasters-work

Types of Energy
https://www.solarschools.net/knowledge-bank/energy/types

INDEX

Oceans of the World

Pacific Ocean

Louise and Richard Spilsbury

heinemann
raintree

Contents

Some words are shown in bold, **like this**. You can find out what they mean by looking in the glossary.

About the Pacific Ocean

The Pacific is one of the world's five oceans. An ocean is a huge area of salty water. The Pacific is the biggest ocean on Earth. It covers about a third of the surface of our planet.

The Pacific Ocean covers more of the surface of Earth than all the dry land put together!

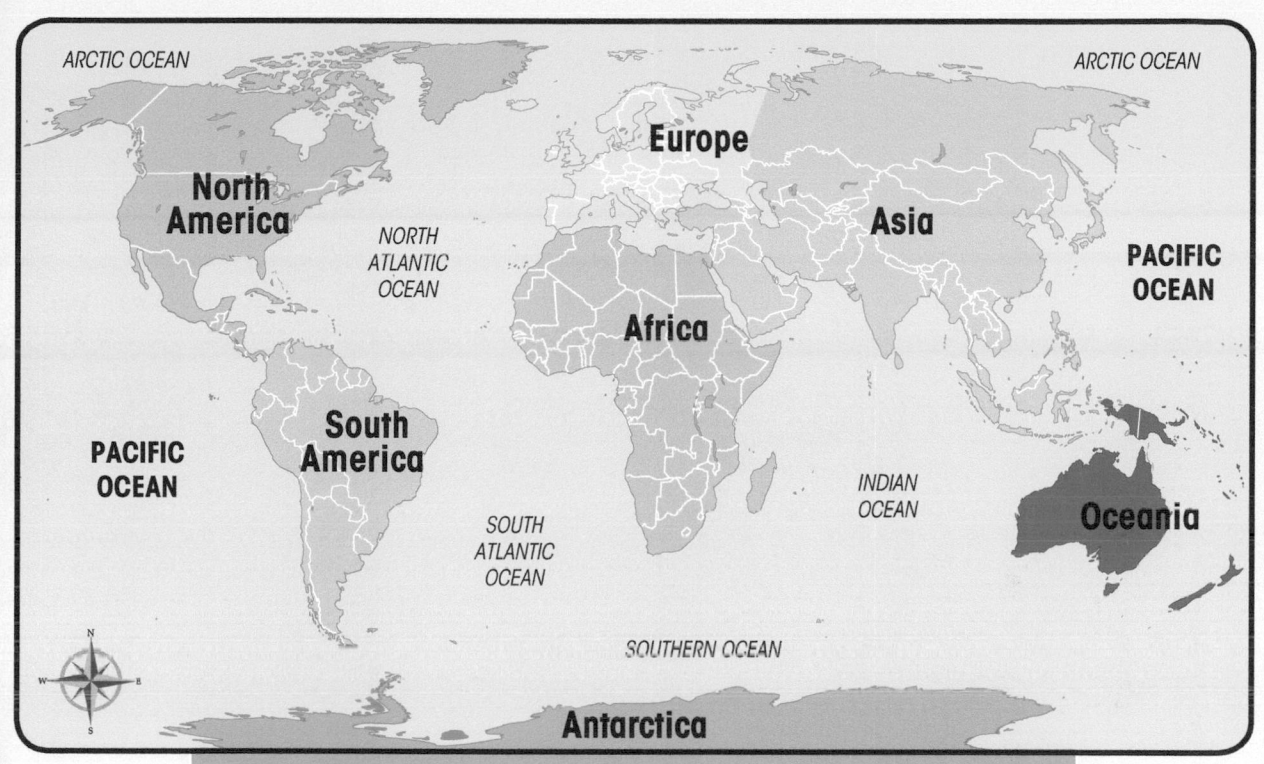

The Pacific Ocean is joined to the other oceans of the world and water flows between them.

The Pacific Ocean stretches from the Arctic Ocean in the north to the Southern Ocean in the south. To the east of the Pacific Ocean lie the **continents** of North America and South America. To the west lie the continents of Asia and Oceania.

An ocean is mostly open water. **Seas** are smaller areas of an ocean found near the land. A sea is also usually partly surrounded by land. The South China Sea, Philippine Sea, Sulu Sea, and Celebes Sea are all part of the Pacific Ocean.

Several seas in the Pacific Ocean lie off the east coast of Asia.

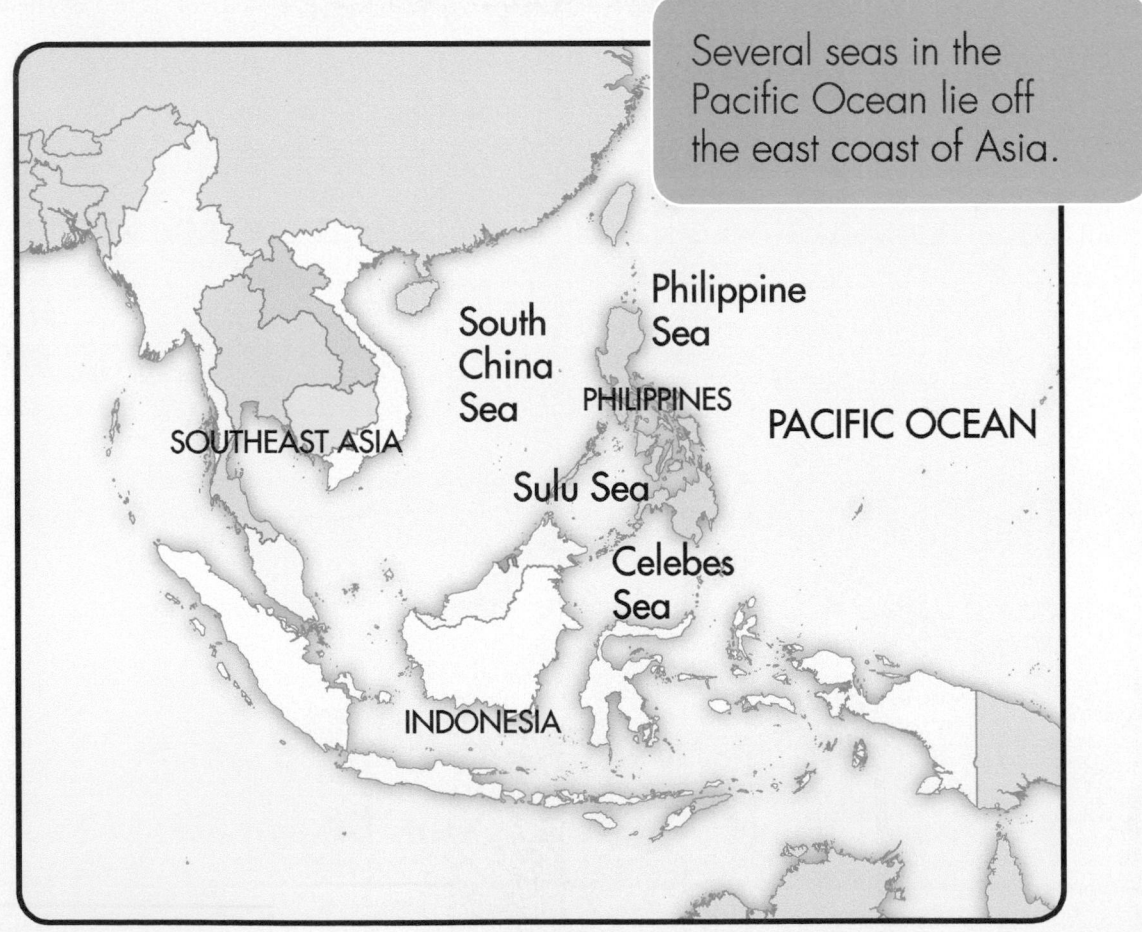

Arctic Ocean

Ships travel through the Bering Strait from the Pacific Ocean to the Arctic Ocean.

Bering Strait

Bering Sea

Pacific Ocean

The Bering Sea is a sea at the far north of the Pacific Ocean. At the top of this sea is the Bering Strait. A **strait** is a narrow corridor of water that links a sea to an ocean.

Geography

The bottom of the ocean has different features, just like the land we live on. In the center of the Pacific, the ocean floor is fairly flat. In some places, there are underwater mountains with steep sides and flat tops. These are called seamounts.

Pacific Ocean fact file	
Surface area (excluding adjacent seas):	63,800,000 square miles (165,250,000 square kilometers)
Average depth:	13,123 feet (about 4,000 meters)
Deepest point:	The Mariana Trench 35,840 feet (10,924 meters) below sea level
Size of the Mariana Trench:	1,580 miles (2,540 kilometers) long and 43 miles (69 kilometers) at the widest point

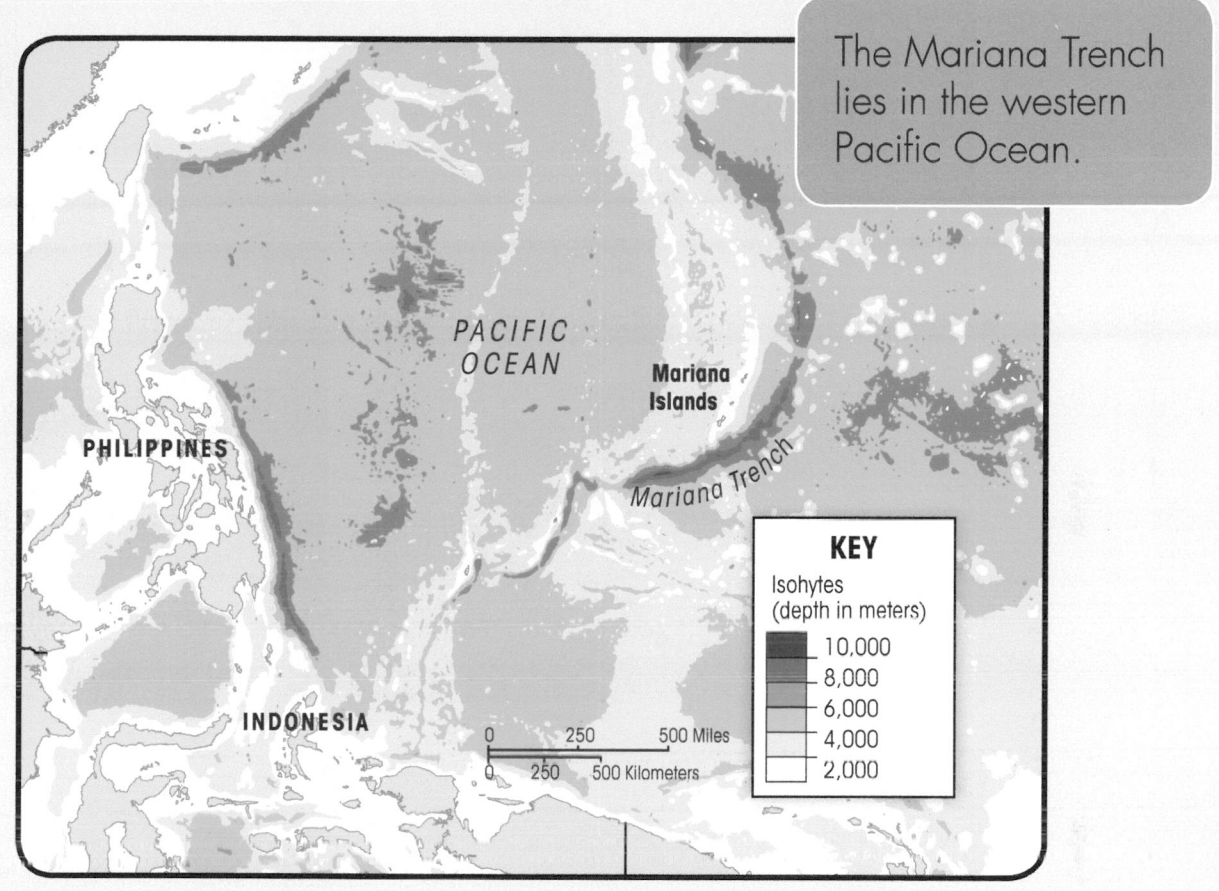

The Mariana Trench lies in the western Pacific Ocean.

PACIFIC OCEAN

Mariana Islands

Mariana Trench

PHILIPPINES

INDONESIA

0   250   500 Miles
0   250   500 Kilometers

KEY

Isohytes
(depth in meters)

10,000
8,000
6,000
4,000
2,000

There are also deep trenches in the Pacific. A trench is a very long, deep, narrow ditch. The biggest Pacific trench is the Mariana Trench. The Challenger Deep in the Marianna Trench is the deepest point on Earth!

The edge of the Pacific Ocean is known as the Ring of Fire because most **volcanoes** are created here. Earth's surface is split into pieces called **plates**. Beneath the Pacific Ocean is the Pacific plate. Volcanoes happen when hot liquid rock from inside Earth rises up in the gap where plates meet.

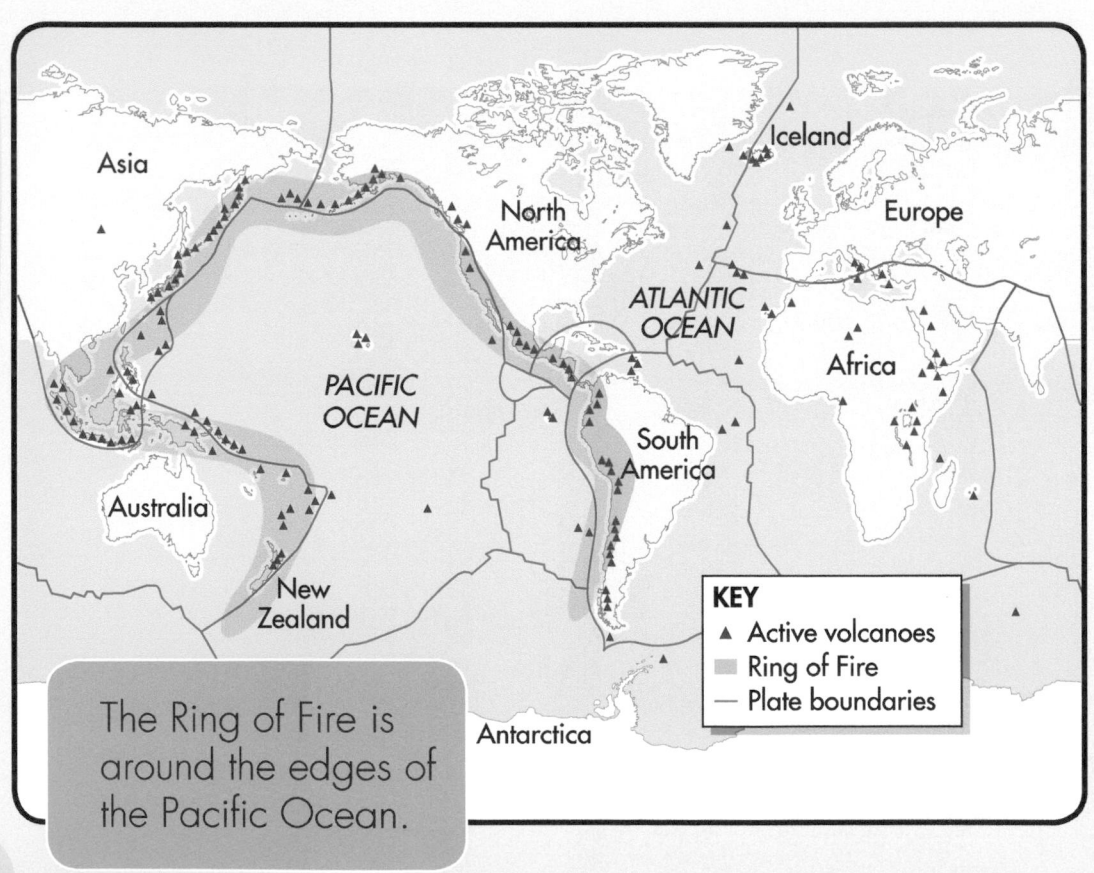

The Ring of Fire is around the edges of the Pacific Ocean.

Giant tsunami waves can crash onto land and cause terrible damage and destruction.

Most of the world's **earthquakes** happen in the Ring of Fire, too. When the Pacific plate scrapes against another plate, the ground shakes and causes an earthquake. When there is an earthquake under the **sea**, this can cause a giant wave called a tsunami.

Temperature

The Pacific Ocean is so big that its water has different temperatures. Near the **Poles** it is very cold, so the water is freezing and can turn to ice. Near the **Equator**, the water in the Pacific Ocean is warmer.

Many tourists visit beaches around the Equator where the waters of the Pacific Ocean are very warm.

This is a satellite picture of a huge hurricane over the Pacific Ocean.

Typhoons or hurricanes sometimes form over the Pacific Ocean. These are huge, whirling winds that happen when warm ocean water heats the air above it. The warm air rises, and this causes winds. When hot air rises quickly, the winds spin very quickly, too.

Islands

There are 25,000 islands in the Pacific, which is more than in any other ocean! An island is an area of land surrounded by water. New Zealand is a country made up of two large islands and many smaller islands in the southwestern Pacific Ocean.

This lovely beach is on North Island, one of New Zealand's two main islands.

The Fijian archipelago is in the South Pacific Ocean.

The country of Fiji is made up of an **archipelago** of different islands. An archipelago is a group or row of islands close together. There are more than 800 islands in Fiji, including over 500 small islands called islets.

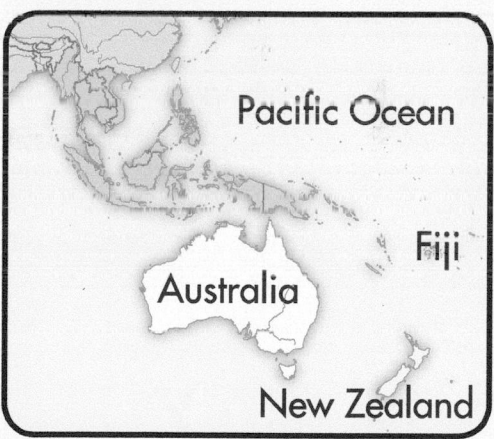

Pacific Ocean

Fiji

Australia

New Zealand

Some Pacific islands are old **volcanoes**. When a volcano **erupts** underwater, the hot, liquid rock cools down quickly and becomes solid rock. The top of this volcanic rock can poke above the water to form an island!

Hawaii

Pacific Ocean

Australia

New Zealand

This island in Hawaii formed from a volcano.

This colorful coral reef is off the coast of the Raja Ampat islands, in Indonesia.

Some volcanic islands in the Pacific Ocean are surrounded by **coral reefs**. Coral is made by millions of tiny animals called polyps. Each polyp builds a skeleton of **limestone** around itself. A coral reef is made of millions of these limestone cases.

Resources

There are lots of useful resources in the Pacific Ocean. People catch more fish here than in any other ocean. In the cold waters of the North Pacific Ocean, big boats called trawlers catch fish such as salmon, tuna, and herring.

Many trawlers have freezers on board to store the caught fish.

People drill for oil under the ocean floor from platforms like these.

People drill under the floor of the Pacific Ocean to get oil and gas. We use these fuels for energy to power vehicles and other machines. People take sand and gravel from the ocean floor for building. They also dig up copper and other metals to make things such as cell phones.

Ports

Lots of ships carry goods and people across the Pacific Ocean. Seattle, Washington, is a city with a big **port** on the west coast of North America. A port is a place where ships load and unload.

Seattle
North America

People can get on a cruise ship in Seattle and travel to Alaska and Canada.

Ships take things made in China across the Pacific to sell all over the world.

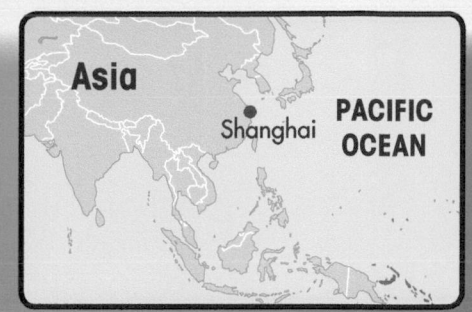

Asia

Shanghai

PACIFIC OCEAN

The port at Shanghai is very busy. Shanghai is a city on the east coast of China. Cranes load containers full of computers, toys, and other goods onto ships.

People

Many people work on the coasts around the Pacific Ocean. In Mexico, there are huge hotels where tourists come to visit the beaches. Many people work here in the hotels, restaurants, and stores.

Some workers take tourists out on boats or on other trips.

Fishing families live in these stilt houses on beaches in the Philippines.

Some people in Washington state live in houseboats on the Pacific Ocean. In the Philippines, some families live in houses on wooden legs called stilts. This keeps the houses dry when the **tide** comes in.

Animals

There are many different animals in the Pacific Ocean. Sea otters live near the coast. They dive to catch clams, crabs, and other small animals underwater. They eat lying on their backs on the water's surface.

Sea otters wrap themselves in seaweed so they don't float away while they sleep!

The giant Pacific octopus can be as big as 30 feet (9 meters) across, when spread out across the ground!

The giant Pacific octopus is the biggest octopus in the world. These amazing animals catch fish, shrimp, and other animals with their long arms. They can change color to hide against rocks on the floor of the Pacific Ocean.

Famous Places

One of the most famous places in the Pacific Ocean is the Great Barrier Reef. This is the biggest **coral reef** in the world. It runs more than 1,250 miles (2,000 kilometers) along the northeast coast of Australia. It contains many beautiful, different-colored corals.

Great Barrier Reef

Australia

Sea turtles, dolphins, and many other amazing animals live on the Great Barrier Reef.

This plastic waste from the Great Pacific Garbage Patch washed up on a beach in Hawaii.

United States

Mexico

Great Pacific Garbage Patch

The Great Pacific Garbage Patch is not beautiful. It is an enormous area of plastic waste floating in the Pacific Ocean. It has been called the biggest garbage dump in the world. Some of the waste is too small to see, but all of it is bad for the ocean and the animals in it.

27

Fun Facts

- The Great Barrier Reef is the only living thing on Earth that astronauts can see from space.

- Over 65 percent of the world's fish caught from the oceans comes from the Pacific Ocean.

- The word "pacific" means "peaceful." The explorer Magellan gave the Pacific Ocean its name because the waters were calm when he first discovered it in 1521.

- If Mount Everest were put into the deepest part of the Mariana Trench, then its top would still be 1.4 miles (2 kilometers) underwater.

- The center of the Pacific Ocean is 1,670 miles (2,688 kilometers) from the nearest land, making it the most remote point on Earth!

Answers

1 The Pacific Ocean is the biggest ocean on Earth.

2 The Mariana Trench is the deepest trench on Earth.

3 The Ring of Fire is where lots of **volcanoes** happen.

4 The Great Pacific Garbage Patch in the Pacific Ocean is the world's biggest garbage dump.

4 Where is the world's biggest garbage dump?

3 Why is the area around the Pacific Ocean called the Ring of Fire?

2 Which is the deepest **trench** on Earth?

1 Which is the biggest ocean on Earth?

Quiz

Glossary

archipelago group or row of islands close together

continent one of seven huge areas of land on Earth

coral reef long line of stony coral rock near the surface of the ocean

earthquake sudden and violent shaking of the ground

erupt when a volcano explodes and hot, melted rock called lava and dust spurt out of it

Equator imaginary line around the middle of Earth

limestone type of hard rock or stone

plate giant piece of rock that floats on the hot rock in the center of Earth

Poles the two points at opposite ends of Earth, the North Pole and South Pole

port place at the edge of an ocean where ships stop

sea smaller area of an ocean usually found near the land and usually partly surrounded by land

strait narrow corridor of water that links seas and oceans

tide way the sea moves up and down the shore twice a day

volcano hole in Earth from which fiery hot, melted rock called lava spurts out

Find Out More

Books

Labrecque, Ellen. *Deep Oceans* (Earth's Last Frontiers). Chicago: Heinemann Library, 2014.

MacQuitty, Miranda. *Ocean* (DK Eyewitness). New York: Dorling Kindersley, 2013.

Newland, Sonya. *Ocean Animals* (Saving Wildlife). Mankato, Minn.: Smart Apple Media, 2012.

Web sites

Facthound offers a safe, fun way to find Internet sites related to this book. All of the sites on Facthound have been researched by our staff.

Here's all you do:
Visit www.facthound.com
Type in this code: 9781484607718

Index